Unveiling the Illusion

Know Who You Are

Dr. Melida A. Harris Barrow

Copyright © 2017, Dr. Melida A. Harris Barrow
All rights reserved.
ISBN 13: 9780998381909
ISBN: 099838190X

No part of this book may be reproduced or transmitted in any form or by any means, electronic or mechanical-including photocopying, recording or by any information storage and retrieval system-without permission in writing from the publisher. Please direct your inquiries to www.unveilingtheillusion.com.

Dedication

To the LOVE of my life, Ambassador of Peace
Felipe Armando Barrow
My sons for giving meaning to my life
Judge Andre Harris IV and Armando Rafael Harris
My grandchildren, blessings from God,
Judge Andre Harris V and Eliza Shea Adkins
My brothers for their unconditional love
Reginaldo F. Johnson and Rodolfo V. Johnson
To my mother and father, Merline M. Davis Johnson
and Reginald Keen Johnson, Thank
you for the gift of life!
Dr. Marcelleus E. Hall,
You made my dream a reality!

Contents

Foreword · vii

Chapter 1 To Be · 1
Chapter 2 God's Space · · · · · · · · · · · · · · · · · · · 11
Chapter 3 Life Power: A Pursuit of Passion · · · · · · · · 23
Chapter 4 Loving Me · 31
Chapter 5 From Pain to Power · · · · · · · · · · · · · · 43
Chapter 6 A Resilient Spirit · · · · · · · · · · · · · · · · 53
Chapter 7 Success · 61

Conclusion · 67
Quotes · 73
Bible Verses · 79
Testimonials · 83
Acknowledgements · · · · · · · · · · · · · · · · 87
Notes · 95

Foreword

There are only two places a person may live, in the reality of that which has been created for them by others or out of the creativeness of their own mind. What a person believes about him or herself to be true cannot be denied by their consciousness and is seen in their footprints throughout time. In order to obtain infinite peace, one must first love themselves enough to acknowledge and embrace the truth about who they are and what they want in this life. In this masterpiece, Dr. Harris-Barrow's work of art is nothing short of phenomenal. In a time where the desperation for change has never been more imminent, "Unveiling the Illusion" provides compassionate enlightenment that is a beacon of light in the darkest corners of the world.

Dr. Melida A. Harris Barrow

Dr. Melida A. Harris Barrow's words reach deep into one's heart, lighting the spark to their soul. She highlights that what we see tainted by our conditioned mindset and how we act based on our given perspective of a situation, "It's all an illusion!" The truth about our current condition is emphasized by bringing reality to light to make well-educated decisions. Ultimately, in life a person reaches absolute success and lives their dreams when they have learned to turn inward and listen to their calling.

I am emotionally moved at the very core of my being by Dr. Harris Barrow's words of benevolence and wisdom. She has feverishly inspired me to move to strike with my pen, bringing to life a force in the form of words introducing her book. A fain attempt that could never measure up in the way she has to me. Honoring me with her wisdom and grace, I was in awe of what I saw as she *unveiled the illusion* to my very own eyes. She is called many things and blessed with so many titles. Yet, I am eternally grateful to have the privilege to introduce her to the people as not only my mentor, but as my spiritual mother.

Dr. Marcellues E. Hall
Colchester, England

Unveiling the Illusion

Know Who You Are

Chapter 1

To Be

Dr. Melida A. Harris Barrow

"To grunt and sweat under a weary life,
But that the dread of something after death-
The undiscover'd country, from whose bourn
No traveller returns- puzzles the will,
And makes us rather bear those ills we have
Than fly to others that we know not of?
Thus conscience does make cowards of us
all, And thus the native hue of resolution
Is sickled o'er with the pale cast of thought,
And enterprises of great pith and moment
With this regard their currents turn awry
And lose the name of action. - Soft you now!"

~ *HAMLET, 1603*

Unveiling the Illusion

When experiencing life, we discover the heartfelt truth of what we cannot control. Hopefully, over time we evolve to the point of understanding the serenity of our decision making; focusing on how we respond to circumstances, rather than how we fall to them. Life happens; it is happening; and it will continue to happen to all of us. Life's inevitable misfortune is that most of what does transpire is seldom, if rarely ever, up to us. Universally speaking, less than often life's events are within our understanding, even less so within our control. That means that the only thing we can control is what we do with our life inherited as moments of time. How ironic is it that the things we have most control over, we exercise authority sparingly? In the end, the inspiration to be great in our lives can be found in a spark from one simple aspiration, our desire "To be"!

From the moment you and I were born into this world, our existence has circumvented within intermittent phases of experiences we cannot control. Good, bad or indifferent, our personal preference is irrelevant. All that life has to offer begins to pile up at our feet. Life proves to be a continuous cycle of recurrent highs and lows. This balance is how the universe and nature works. Yet, in realizing that suffering is only temporary, we unveil our opportunity to make something positive out of any negative situation. However, this thought process and way of thinking can only be developed when you first understand the balance of experiencing life is focusing on your actions, or "To be".

Although undesirable events will occur in life, they do not have to define you or permanently impair your growth. Only the belief there is nothing you can do about your situation will limit your potential for greatness. The only absolute and indefinite limitations in life are those self-imposed. You may not always favor your options, but you do have a choice! This is your life's journey, and you must experience it.

> As a revolutionary poet once stated: *"If you do not learn to become an artist painting the art of your life, all you will ever be is a picture of what you once were, or could have been."*
>
> ~ GYPSY POET

You have "To be"! Living life is when you take the proactive approach to opportunities in life. This is the moment when you become the "creator" of your destiny-*the second you choose to make demands within your life.* It is the conscious decision of how you will live regardless of what someone else says, thinks, or feels about your choices. Not everyone on this Earth will choose to live life. Many will only experience it, expecting no more than what has been given to them. They will accept whatever has been handed to them without question or aspirations to do anything elevating themselves above their current situation. These are the ones who will settle, telling themselves, "This is the best I can do." Despite amassing wealth and possessions, you can still be enslaved to the same psychological conditioning as someone who has accumulated very little in life. The only difference is that often a rich person with a conditioned mind is more socially acceptable than a poor person with a conditioned mind. Coincidently, they both spend their time alone, wishing they were someone or somewhere else.

Living life is seen in those who choose to demand first of themselves, then of others. These people have awakened to the change they wish to create. This small community of individuals within our enormous world will dare to be different. Now bear in mind, I am not saying it will be easy. What I am saying is that if you truly want to be the creative master of your life, you will have to do what is necessary to make it happen. Unfortunately, this involves doing the one thing most people hate to do the most, suffer! Yes, in those times we must remember, pain is only the beginning of many wondrous things. After all, life is a process. Never let the idea of suffering keep you from being who you want to be. You want to get to the point in your life that no matter what happens, how many setbacks you encounter or how much it hurts, "To be" will no longer be a question, but a state of mind representing the essence of who you truly are!

Some circumstances will make it harder than others. There will also be people who will tell you what you can and cannot achieve in your life. In these times you must ask yourself, do you define your life based on their lack of understanding or belief in your capabilities? How can they possibly know your limits when they do not know their own? People will tell you that you cannot achieve something, especially when it is something they cannot do themselves or at least have never seen done before. If you can survive the psychological and emotional opposition, what remains is nothing less than greatness! I encourage you to embrace the suffering in the challenges you face as you grow into yourself. Pain is only temporary and the beginning of things in life. The struggle you endure is what divine success feels like. Life is not measured by the destination of the road traveled, but the strength and courage to meet the road upon which one travels towards their desired destination.

> *"I believe there is a deeper level of consciousness breached and vibrations felt when we communicate at elevated levels above climates set by those in positions of authority. Normally in our day-to-day lives, unavailable to us because of societies*

psychological fabrications, these experiences challenge and transcend our standard way of thinking. It is as if our clarity is distorted, seeing upside down with a sideways perspective, trapped inside Gods mythical prism. There are times I feel so connected to everything and everyone around me that I literally feel the vibrations from the kiss of nature dismount her lips and invade mine. I can feel the way I am loved or unwanted simply by the frequency of the pulse and the intensity of a heartbeat. Searching for the demand in someone's eyes, life sometimes can feel as if I am soul shopping. I feel the vibration of every life force of energy passing me by."

~ Dr. M. Hall

It is in nature that God meets with man. A title isn't needed to establish your greatness. You are already great! You can feel your greatness in the energy of the world around you. There is a level of consciousness and understanding between man and nature. Yet, man will tell you without a title you have not fulfilled the requirements necessary to be considered what it is that you want to be. For example, it does not take a Master's Degree in Art for you to become an artist. The moment you begin to draw freely upon your imagination, pulling from the inspiration of the universe, you were an artist. You do not become an artist so that you can learn to draw. On the contrary, you are an artist and that energy is what you draw from and why you draw.

The piece of paper (certificate) that gives you a title is a tool used in a market for which it was designed by those who control it. Man has leased the land from nature and claimed it for themselves. Creating titles 'they say' are required to access greatness, but God is saying, " You were already born great. Who will you believe?" History is full of great authors, poets, musicians and other forms of professions that attended man's great institutions to become such. However, these institutions are nothing more than just that, an institution that was created to reconstruct the way man thinks. Now, I am not saying that getting additional knowledge from schools is not necessary. But, what I am saying they are not necessary to access your greatness. Learning institutions help you develop upon your greatness, but they do not define it, nor do they create it. Your greatness in life, in anything that you decide to do, can only come from within when you decide "To be" great. We should never let any man hold the *key* for us to access something that can only come from within us, and that is our greatness that comes from God!

Unveiling the Illusion

"How can you thank a man for giving you something that is already yours!"

~ Malcolm X

Do not wait for man to add value to your life. You will be lost for the rest of your life while waiting on someone to give your existence purpose. Your life is not increased or decreased in value based on the accolades man believes you deserve. Part of the illusion is that many people today still believe there is a checklist that needs to be completed before they can be considered accomplished. The accomplishments in your life are based on your goals set for life by you. No one can add value to that or take it away. No one should define who you are, only you can do that. We must reset the way we think. Return to our original self before being conditioned by man's purpose for our life. You must tell yourself the 'I am that I am' created me to be Great!

I am often reminded of a story about an elephant in Africa. For several years it lived its life on his belly tied down to a pole. So afraid to stand up because society has put in his head that he is weak. For many years it stayed there; tied down and oppressed. One day the elephant did something it never dared to do before, it looked up. As long as the elephant kept his eyes toward the sky, it began to lift its trunk to the heavens. Slowly he felt a shift in the ground that began to shake his spirit. He felt the ground break and dared to do the impossible; he stood up. As he stood, the pole came out of the Earth. The elephant was free! Yet, the elephant stood there puzzled with a look on his face. He noticed something; he was not tied down. The elephant was naturally and spiritually crippled for several years because man tied him down and made him believe he didn't have the strength to break free. He believed man knew more about his strength, courage and intelligence than he did.

You must realize that our heaviest burdens are those self-imposed. The elephant did not need man to loosen the ropes so that he can access his greatness; he was already great because he was born great. It is imperative that we are "To be" in order to achieve our greatness. Waiting on man is like suffocating or holding our breath until someone tells us to breathe. Why wait on man to give you something that is not theirs to give in the first place? Be as you were born "To be"… BOUNDLESSLY GREAT!

Chapter 2

God's Space

Dr. Melida A. Harris Barrow

"Energy is neither created nor destroyed, it can only be changed from one form to another."

~ Albert Einstein

Unveiling the Illusion

The absolute law of conservation energy states that energy is neither created nor destroyed. Extensive thermodynamics research (*physics concerned with heat and temperature and their relation to energy and work*) has shown that unless energy is interrupted by an outside force it remains constant. If the forces of the universe obey this law, then how true is this law for us as human beings? Is the constant harmony of this energy system at peace within the human soul disrupted by outside forces as well? Over the years, I found this to be the absolute truth. When encountered by negativity, it causes distortion to the cerebral cortex that travels down the spine thus affecting the physical body. This universal space of ours, I like to call "God's Space" must be protected at all times by being cautious of the energy we allow in our life from outside forces and people.

Do you recall a time sitting in a room feeling total peace within yourself regardless of your current situation? Suddenly, someone changes the atmosphere from their presence or conversation. The vibe from this person is so disturbing that you find yourself mentally or spiritually drained. Some people call this intuition. For those that believe in the Astrologer's chart, Cancerians are noted for being sensitive to the energy of others. They are known for having great intuition and are vulnerable to others energy around them. In fact, Cancers can be quite moody. Just thinking about a person can alter their state of being.

Dr. Melida A. Harris Barrow

You see this is what happens when we invite people into our lives and allow them to take up God's space. Our mood changes when we allow our thoughts and feelings to be consumed by other people's problems and negativity. The peace you once had is no more. Interrupted by an outside source, our energy shifts, thus enabling our mood to become bitter, angry, depressed and unresolved. So we must always protect God's space by being vigilant and selective of the company we keep!

> *"[10] Finally, be strong in the Lord and in his great power. [11] Put on the full armor of God so that you can fight against the devil's evil tricks. [12] Our fight is not against people on earth but against the rulers and authorities and the powers of this world's darkness, against the spiritual powers of evil in the heavenly world. [13] That is why you need to put on God's full armor. Then on the day of evil you will be able to stand strong. And when you have finished the whole fight, you will still be standing. [14] So stand strong, with the belt of truth tied around your waist and the protection of right living on your chest. [15] On your feet wear the Good News of peace to help you stand strong. [16] And also use the shield of faith with which you can stop all the burning arrows of the Evil One.*

> *[17] Accept God's salvation as your helmet, and take the sword of the Spirit, which is the word of God. [18] Pray in the Spirit at all times with all kinds of prayers, asking for everything you need. To do this you must always be ready and never give up. Always pray for all God's people."*
>
> ~ EPHESIANS 6:10-18 *(NCV)*

We are soldiers on a battlefield. Our greatest weapon is maintaining our positive energy. This is better known as "*positive reinforcement*". With a positive attitude we can balance our feelings and emotions, shaping our perception of what we see in life. We are what we think we are. We must be cognizant of our attitude that we release from the very moment our eyes open each morning. Therefore, it is of the utmost importance to guard your mind and prepare your spirit every day for what you may face. Why? There will be many interferences that will attempt to invade your space.

God's spirit is more than just empty space floating around the universe. It is your body (temple), the inner vessel that carries your soul throughout this lifetime. Like any vessel, it can be filled with the debris-*other people's issues*. Protecting that positive energy begins with monitoring whose energy you allow to enter your vessel. As the bible urges us, we must arm ourselves with the entire armor of GOD! More importantly, if you are going to open yourself up to God and be anointed with His blessings, you have to make sure that there is space available for you to be filled. Space available for God to work through you and positively influence the people entrusted to you. That space is the foundation from which we pull our resources to accomplish our mission here in this life. We have to remember that is God's space!

To gain a deeper understanding of God's space, picture a vessel of water. That water is the source of purity and life abundance. Inside that vessel full of water lies the key ingredients to preserving life. The more space available in that vessel, the more water you can place into the vessel. With that water, life is purified and assists in maintaining your very existence. Now, imagine this same vessel of water, but it has mud and dirt taking up space. The more mud and dirt you have in your vessel; the less room you have for water. More importantly, the water is tainted and diluted by the debris from the mud and dirt. That water can no longer fulfill its purpose. Instead of the water preserving life, it diminishes life. This water can even make you sick and die!

God and fear cannot occupy the same space; neither can light nor darkness. You cannot have your vessel full of negativity and produce positivity simultaneously. They cannot exist occupying the same space. So, what do you suppose happens when we allow our hearts, consciousness, and souls to be infiltrated and infused with the negativity of the world and the people in it? We begin to perform half quality work and our focus is off centered to any given task. What God intended for our lives is now hindered or impaired. Why? Our vessels are filled with things that are counterproductive to our goals and purpose in life. The importance of safeguarding our hearts and minds could not be more critical. If we do not protect our temple, we will be transformed through manipulation and distortion of other people's energy, thus preventing us from fulfilling our purpose.

> *And lately I wonder if you have*
> *Been trying to tell me something*
> *We used to talk all night and*
> *do things alone together*
> *And I have begun (as a reaction to feeling)*
> *To balance the pain of loneliness*
> *against the pain of loving you!*

~ GIOVANNI, 1943

Nikki Giovanni is saying that we need to balance the lies (illusion) from the truth. The pain of loneliness along with the pain of loving you is overcasting the reality that we don't talk anymore. It has invaded my space. People lives are spent living for someone other than themselves. We allow their issues and problems to occupy space that should have been reserved for God. Matter of fact, most of our issues in life come from dealing with someone else's baggage, not our own. Over a period of a time, we do more damage to ourselves than anyone else can ever do to us. Our power is given away, not stolen. In order to reserve this space for God within our vessel, we have to restructure our thinking. Be aware of the company you keep and how you engage with them.

> *"The Law of Attraction can be understood by understanding that 'like attracts like'. What this means is that whether we realize it or not, we are responsible for bringing both positive and negative influences into our lives. A key part of the Law of Attraction is understanding that where you place your focus can have an intense impact on what happens to you. If you spend your days wallowing in regrets about the past or fears of the future, you'll likely see more negativity appearing, but if you look for the silver lining in every experience then you'll soon start to see positivity will surround you every day. Therefore, the Law of*

Unveiling the Illusion

Attraction encourages you to see that you have the freedom to take control of how your futures develops, shaping it in the ways you choose."

~ Hurst, 2016

We may not always create the positive and negative energy that comes to us in our lives, but we do attract it by engaging with these forces with our thoughts. When you constantly think negative and imagine the worst outcome for a scenario, negativity is usually what we get. Reshaping our thoughts and thinking process enables us to tune into the positive things in our lives. This does not mean negative things will not happen. There is nothing we can do to keep a storm from invading our lives at times, but how we react in the midst of the storm is up to us. We have a choice as to how we will respond despite the situation or circumstance. There is so much power within us. We must choose wisely what we will allow to penetrate our space (God's space).

You were not created to make "*man*" happy. The bible speaks about how a man cannot serve two masters, he must love one and hate the other. Be sure that you have room in your heart to fulfill your desires and the desires of God. God's space must constantly be replenished as you continue to work towards your goal in life. You have to realize the dangers of trying to please everyone around you. So many of us grow weary trying to please everyone, but ourselves and God. Then, we wonder why we are not successful or happy with what we have acquired? Whether rich or poor, we are given a few options as to what we will be in life. Our lives are guided by our parents, teachers and peers. Despite the influence, this is your life, not theirs. Only you can live the life that God has purposed for you to live.

Another factor in how we manage God's space with others; is the relationship mutually beneficial? Many of us find ourselves in a one-sided romance. We put everything 'on the line' and never get anything in return. We have to question ourselves, what do we get back in return from the energy we give out? There is no mutual exchange. That is not satisfying. In fact, it is discouraging.

What are you filling your space with? This is a very important question. If you are not careful, your fairytale will be a prequel to a horror story. We hear it all the time, know your worth! Once you have decided what you believe you are worth, do not accept anything less. To ensure you are receiving what you need from a partner, job, or any outside source; be sure to reflect on the relationship. Make sure that the exchange is mutually beneficial. Why? Because the gift God has given you, is priceless.

Do not be afraid to remove yourself from negative forces or people that do not contribute positively to your life. If the exchange is not mutually beneficial, do not engage with it. Staying positive and protecting God's space is critical to achieving your life's purpose. It is what you were born to do!

A soldier trains for war by becoming a better soldier than his enemy. An athlete trains to perform better than his challenger. The same goes for us in everyday life. Accomplishing this task means you have to be driven to do better than your opponent. Do not consume yourself with negative energy from others-*stay the course*. Protect your space – God's space!

Audre Lorde said, "If I did not learn to define myself for myself, I would be crunched into other's fantasies for me and eaten alive." Do not give your power away. So many of us hand our power over to others. We allow what someone says to or about us to affect our state of mind. We have relinquished our power over to them. Live your life and fulfill your purpose. This is why you are here! I remember hearing my elders say, "It is not what they call you; it is what you answer to." Do not cast your pearls before swine. Reserve space for your positivity; reserve space for growth; reserve space for you; and most importantly, reserve space for GOD!

Chapter 3

Life Power: A Pursuit of Passion

Dr. Melida A. Harris Barrow

"My mission in life is not merely to survive, but to thrive; and to do so with some passion, some compassion, some humor, and some style."

~ Maya Angelou

Unveiling the Illusion

There is a power within us all that is not of this world. All of us are God's children and have been given a calling with a purpose in life. Everyone wants to know, "What is my purpose?" This question is startling when you do not know who you are. Your purpose is greater than any purpose that can come from man. Discover what you were born to do and pursue it with an endless passion that burns hotter than any flame known to man.

It is not enough to simply exist. There is something deeper that inspires us to want to do better. Here is the problem: our passion is up for sale in a market that can profit from us. We are constantly compared to something or someone else. When we do not measure up to someone else's standards, we begin to question our purpose. The only comparison you should have is the person looking back at you in the mirror. Your purpose cannot be decided by man. We have to get back to having that one-on-one personal relationship with God. It is there that we hear God. His spirit then speaks to us whispering in our ears and gently touching our hearts.

It is so important to acknowledge and believe that our life powers and pursuit of passion comes from the God of this universe. It is a gift from Him. If you do not understand that God is the sole provider of your strength and power, then you can find yourself feeling insignificant unless someone gives you something to have authority over.

Dr. Melida A. Harris Barrow

We have the power to create, build, and change things in this world. It needs to start with our personal lives. This power of life is a great power. You must learn to understand it and apply its resource to embark on your journey. You cannot know where you are going, if you do not know where you are from.

Follow your passion; be prepared to work hard and sacrifice; and, above all, never allow anyone limit your dreams (Donovan Bailey). There are many of us who give our power away and slowly our passion for life diminishes with it. When you don't understand you are the *key*, you believe someone else unlocks the doors of opportunities. This mentality causes one to depend on others to 'make things happen for us'. As a result of this mentality, society defines who we are, what we are capable of and ultimately guides the outcome of our life.

In the 1960s Fred Hampton sat down with men from a bank who were looking to put a Credit Union in African American neighborhoods. The first thing he asked for was information involving the education program. Mr. Hampton made a very powerful statement when he said, "Without education the people are nowhere. People will begin to steal from us (the credit union) because they do not understand its value and why it belongs to the people." If you do not know why you are doing what you are doing, you are likely to miss its intended purpose, and never contribute to the cause. Furthermore, if we do not have the passion to achieve our life's purpose, we do not experience fulfillment of life.

> *"Growing up, I was inspired by what I had seen in my community. I didn't want other people to go through what I went through in my home. There were many arguments and fights at home; but I had a loving grandmother. She gave me the balance to love. The love I have today, I owe to my grandmother. She always told me I was a Queen and that I would speak to the world. At age eleven, I started going to church in the neighborhood. It was at church that I was inspired to teach. My pastor said I was always running my mouth with the other kids. So he gave me a position as a Sunday School teacher. That's when I started going to different communities with my pastor teaching."*
>
> ~ Dr. Harris Barrow

The power to life is not seeking it, but realizing it already exists within you. Learning to make things happen with what you already have available to you is an important life lesson. We were born with the necessary tools to be successful and powerful in life. I always knew there was something special in me. Even though I did not know exactly what it was, I knew there was a divine purpose for my life. I did not know what it was, but I knew it was connected to God. As a child, helping people became natural, Today, I acknowledge and recognize my God given purpose and have passionately embraced it.

You have to be careful when listening to people about your life's purpose and passion. We can easily become distracted by people telling us what we should be doing. It is known you can do anything you put your mind to. However, if it is not what you're called to do, the lack of passion will nullify life's fulfillment. Stay committed to what you enjoy! Stay committed to your passion and gift. Doing this will elevate you to unknown heights which allows you to elevate others. When we are empowered, the next step will be empowering others.

Learning what is your life's fulfillment is extremely important. For me, my life's fulfillment is helping others. You cannot put a price tag on assisting people become a better version of themselves. When someone comes to thank me for helping them maximize their potential, it is the greatest reward one could ever receive. I have dedicated my life's work to passionately serving others.

> "I have always been able to sense pain. So, when I recognize pain, I help people. It is such a joy to watch someone turn their light on. The sense of helping people is a joy for me. When I help them, I help myself. The more joy I give, the better I feel."
>
> ~ Dr. Harris Barrow, 2015

When living out your life's purpose, never settle. The initial reaction or response to hearing the word "settle" can appear synonymous to giving up, or no longer willing to act in favor of one's wishes. Before anyone states the obvious, let me address the ultimate contradiction. Settling does not always present a submissive nature. For some individuals, settling in life is only considered after achieving one's aspired goals or desires originally sought. On the other hand, after reaching one's milestone, the alternative state of mind that the majority of the human race has, is 'settling'.

Dr. Melida A. Harris Barrow

Many people will settle for less in reference to a person, circumstance, or outcome in their life because they do not believe it is possible to *exceed* their previous performance. Others will settle because they cannot envision anything beyond what they currently hold in their possession. The fact of the matter is that most people will not choose a height worthy of great ascent, due to limitations they place on themselves. The mental condition circumventing this thought process is not only disheartening, but has vastly become the inherited mindset of our current generation. Limited thinking creates a society of dependent, directed and unreliable minds. If not addressed properly, it will deteriorate the very fabric of our individuality, personal desire and most important of all, humanity. We have to remember that we were placed here on this Earth to do great things. We come from a mighty God. Settling is not an option. Live your life's purpose!

Chapter 4

Loving Me

"Perhaps we will learn, as we pass through this age, that the other self" is more powerful than the physical self we see when we look into the mirror."

~ NAPOLEON HILL, *THINK AND GROW RICH*

Unveiling the Illusion

The word love is probably one of, if not the most popular and verbally used word known to mankind. Rarely will you find another word used so figuratively and passionately, yet loosely. To say this word is used lucidly would be inaccurate because most people do not know what it means to love. This is usually because they do not know how to love themselves. Love is gentle, kind, and true. Most importantly, love is unconditional!

For me, love is the true essence of life! It can be seen in all things surrounding us. From the tears falling from heaven to water the Earth replenishing her roots, you will find love. When the wind blows across the lands at the foot of the hills you will find love. Yes, it is true that love can be seen in so many things around us daily. Sadly, love is rarely seen in the one place that our success and happiness requires we witness it the most, ourselves.

What is it that we see when we look into the mirror? Is it beauty, intelligence, strength or ambition? How you love yourself, is more likely than not, determines how you interpret yourself. What you see in yourself is a perceived notion that stems from what you think about yourself. That's it! Furthermore, who taught you to think this way? That is a significant inquiry that demands to be answered. It is true, your soul (the real self) is more powerful than the physical self, when we are looking into the mirror. It is most vital that we validate the love we see in the mirror is our own, not an illusion of love, that society has instilled in your mind.

> "*¹²Now we see things imperfectly, like puzzling reflections in a mirror, but then we will see everything with perfect clarity. All that I know now is partial and incomplete, but then I will know everything completely, just as God now knows me completely. ¹³Three things will last forever-faith, hope and love- and the greatest of these is love."*
>
> *~ 1 Corinthians 13: 12-13 (NLT)*

Unconditional love is the fundamental building block to knowing the importance of how it affects our everyday lives. Having this divine revelation of unconditional love will show us how to love in spite of circumstances that would persuade our hearts to do differently. Most people love someone or something when it benefits them. When the person or thing that we love disappoints or hurts us, the love stops. We don't love anymore. Love, in this instance, is measured by its ability to benefit and maintain control. That is not unconditional love; it is love based on conditions. Unfortunately, this is the way most people love.

Unveiling the Illusion

Imagine a child who decides one day that he wants to learn how to box. He watches television and imagines himself being the next champion, like Floyd Mayweather.

At the time, he does not realize that his love for the sport is nothing more than a fascination. He does not know the extent of time, commitment, and sacrifice that has been dedicated to the sport. One day, the boy has a boxing match and wins. That evening he tells his mother how much he loves the game! Boxing match after boxing match, the young man wins. His love for the game grows immensely that he cannot imagine himself doing anything else. Now, he meets his match. The young man has a boxing match with an opponent who is just as strong, committed, and willing to sacrifice as much as he is. He gets hit hard. Every punch hurts more and more than the one before. Eventually, the boy decides he does not want to fight any more and quits. After the fight is over, the young man spirit is broken. He vows never to fight again after losing that fight. He tells his mother he does not love the sport after all and wants to do something else.

Does this sound familiar? This is the way most people love. Like the young man, when things are going well, he loved what he was doing. The moment life hit him back and he felt the sting from its mighty blow, his heart changed. Simply stated, as long as you are winning, making money and it feels good, you want to continue doing what are doing. However, the mind and heart changes as soon as 'life's blows' and knocks the wind from you. Think about this, your spouse decides he or she does not like a particular activity you once celebrated together. Business is not progressing and you are required to work weekends for the next six months. Hmmm, life has lost its spark. What you once adored is requiring much sacrifice. Due to the sacrifice, you do not feel the same way about what you are doing as you once did. Your passion is not burning so hot and the light has dimmed on your dream. You realize the thrill is gone.

The truth is you never loved what you were doing. You were in love with the idea of being successful, making money, etc. But, you did not want to suffer. Suffering demands sacrifice. In life you are going to have to prove how much you love something even when the odds are not in your favor. You did not love what you were doing unconditionally. You loved under the conditions that what you were doing was benefiting you and you were winning. In other words, it was under the illusion that society teaches: *when someone or something contests our desires they do not love us.* When it comes to things you love and it's not your favor, you quit!

> *"I am so glad that God does not quit on us! What if God loved under conditions? Can you imagine*

Unveiling the Illusion

how difficult life would be for us? Despite all of our imperfections and shortcomings, we are still loved unconditionally by God. The unconditional love and favor of God exemplifies the importance of love. Because without it, we would all be lost."

~ Dr. Marcellues Hall

How beautiful God is and I mean this sincerely. Despite our actions against his divine will and continuous decisions we make that hurt us, God still loves us. It does not matter that we have made a thousand mistakes, our Creator knows we are going to make a thousand more. Yet, he blesses and loves us the same! How amazingly wonderful life would be if we loved each other that way? Despite our physical differences or personal preferences, we choose to love unconditionally. Throughout history, the indifference between men tends to lead to violence, hate, and all-out war. We are at a pivotal low-point in society. We lack respect and love for one another as unique individuals. When we look at our shameful past, the demand for unconditional love has never been greater.

Have you ever thought to ask yourself why unconditional love is so important? If you take a moment to analyze the world around you, what is it that you see? In the four corners of the world, you will see endless accounts of suffering in forms of discrimination, racism, poverty, economic enslavement, overbearing political reform from controlling governments and extremely high levels of incarceration rates! What is it that provokes mankind to be so demanding, cruel and hateful? In our world today, it would appear that it is more natural for man to hurt one another than to love one another. This is not what God had in mind for us when we were created. How did we get here and where is the love?

Since the laws of physics tell us that energy does not manifest itself anew, it is neither created nor destroyed. It is transferred from one state to another. Where does the hate come from? It is an accepted study that hatred is learned behavior. Studies show that children are not born racist or hating one another because of their differences. This behavior is learned over time from the observation of others. Likewise, if we can learn to hate then we can learn to love. Even more so, love comes naturally. Love has the ability to eradicate hate just like light dispels darkness.

Now that we know the origin of hate, how do we get to the unconditional love? First, we must understand whose we are. We are created in the image of God's love for us. It is not enough to understand what is happening around us. There are reasons why things are happening in our lives; it is much deeper than what we see in the present moment. For example, if your reality is that others are superior to you, then your life experiences will be one of disappointments, hurts, pain and suffering. In fact, it's human nature to control or become master over someone. It is not until that person believes and accepts this belief for themselves, that they begin to truly suffer. Jean-Jacques Rousseau says, "Man is born free, and everywhere he is in chains. One man thinks himself the master of others, but remains more of a slave than they are." If what you've been told has now become a thought-process, then consider your offspring. Our future generation cannot be under the same thumbprint of oppression. Move away from the illusion and love yourself unconditionally.

Loving yourself unconditionally cannot be expressed enough. It is the foundation of everything in your life that is great. All that we do and achieve in life begin with loving yourself, as well as, knowing the truth about who you are! You must remove yourself from the illusion that you are inferior or less than great. It all starts with you. No one knows your skills and abilities better than you do. When you see the greatness that God has given you, it is then you notice your worth. When you are true to yourself, then *and only then*, will you be able to rise to the top and fulfill your life's purpose. On the contrary, when you do not love or believe in yourself, limitations are placed on your life. We do more damage to ourselves than anyone can ever do. In the words of Shakespeare, "To thine own self be true".

Unconditional love is not only a necessity for you to love yourself, but for you to help and love your family and friends as well. You cannot help anyone until you help yourself. This is a phrase that we have heard countless times before and it is as valid today as it was back then. There isn't anything wrong with taking time to make your situation in life better as long as you help someone else along the way. The greatest resource is not money, jewelry or wealth. The greatest resource is the unconditional love that is extended to others once we mastered it ourselves. When we love unconditional, we are willing to go the extra mile to see the good in others. There are no limits with unconditional love. It is your strength beyond strength and will be needed in every aspect of your life.

> *"And we have known and believed the love that God hath to us. God is love, and he that dwelleth in love, dwelleth in God, and God in him."*
>
> ~ 1 JOHN 4:16 (KJV)

Dr. Melida A. Harris Barrow
(Unveiled The Illusion Physically & Mentally)

Do not be conformed to this world, but be transformed by the renewing of your mind, so that you may prove what the will of God is, that which is good and acceptable and perfect.

~ Romans 12:2 (NIV)

Age 35   Age 56

Chapter 5

From Pain to Power

*Those who believe suffering last forever
Will forever suffer.
There is no reason to suffering, no cause
to suffering, no End to suffering
Embrace the suffering
The only easy day was yesterday
Pain is only the beginning
This is what success feels like.*

~ UNKNOWN

Unveiling the Illusion

Where does pain begin? Better yet, when does it end? The pain of suffering is weighing on the hearts and minds of so many people, which keep their spirits in bondage. Because of this suffering, people lack peace and are unable to see the truth of God's love that can lead them to better days. The mind has been captivated which makes it difficult to escape the pain of life's uncertainties. This illusion of the mind is the deadliest disease one can have. When your mind is not right, the world around you is distorted. When you acknowledge who you are, *aligning yourself with God's purpose for your life*, there is nothing stopping you from activating the power from within.

Society has spread this illusion that your happiness is something that they are born in pursuit of, rather than in possession of. Our global leaders, economic dictators, and market analysts wants you to believe there is something greater in their world than the joy in your world. Our minds are robbed blind as we hold on to a glimmer of light they offer us in exchange for pursuing and sacrificing our own dreams. Fulfilling our God given purpose may cause us to suffer. It's time to 'unveil the illusion' and know who you are and your capabilities.

At times, we forget we are a powerful people. We are born to win! There is no need for a pursuit of happiness when it has already been given by the God of the Universe. The suffering that we endure is not because we failed at happiness. On the contrary, we merely lack the truth! Ironically, we never step outside 'the box' for the truth. We stay within the perimeters dictated to us by mankind-*society*.

Society has depicted a picture of reality that is an 'illusion'. It saddens me that men are in mental and or spiritual bondage. Regardless of birthplace, social class or social order, they are bound with an illusion. Their 'reality' lacks merit and truth. Nothing can be given to you when it is already a part of who you are. You determine your happiness. No one, *I mean no one*, can control or determine your happiness.

Think about Christmas time. Each Christmas we spend precious time with our families. We have unforgettable memories that cannot be erased. However, society wants us to embrace the belief that if we do not participate in the global economic boost for various companies, we lack holiday spirit. Never mind there is no reality in such a claim (holiday spirit). It's all about enhancing the company's wealth. Parents work overtime to buy their children toys and electronics they do not need. They even go into debt because of their commitment to society's definition of happiness. To add salt to an open wound, Christmas morning you do not receive any credit for the sacrifices of working overtime to make someone else happy. Credit goes to a white beard man in a red suit riding through the sky with nine reindeers – *Dasher, Dancer, Prancer, Vixen, Comet, Cupid, Donder, Blitzen and Rudolph*. He slides down a chimney, eating special treats left behind, only to ride off into the night. Really…What an Illusion? The reality is that your purses and wallets are lighter because of this white bearded man.

Even though we realize Santa Claus is a lie, we lack holiday spirit if we do not submit to this man made tradition. In fact, we are criticized for not participating in this illusion. Although we know this 'tall tale' does not make sense, we yet do it because it brings happiness to children. Look, when there is peace and love in the home, a child would be happy playing in a cardboard box. We suffer so much because we fail to acknowledge the truth. We chase a lifestyle whether we believe in it or not.

We do more harm to ourselves by self-inflicting unnecessary pain and suffering. The precarious situations that we place ourselves in do more emotional, mental, financial, and spiritual damage than we can imagine. As if we are in love with a lie, rather than the truth. How do we begin to transform our minds and elevate ourselves above this way of thinking? First, examine how we process information. Observe the situation and not out of association from past experiences. Evaluation is absolute! Anything or anyone subjected to being analyzed is often defined based on subjective and bias information from a social-economic perspective. We have to stop comparing ourselves to false images and see clearly who we are and what we can become.

What we have available to us to analyze any situation is based on our limited understanding; yet, we call this informed decision-making. Thus, all that we know is in part. A final and absolute decision about who we are, cannot be adjudged in total confidence by a mind that is not properly educated (if educated at all) about who we are. Partially conscious and selectively informed by what is made available is usually the foundation of what we are led to believe.

What is this false sense of self that has taken hold to our minds? When will we awaken to the infinite possibility of who we are? Our pain is only temporary, but we cannot relieve ourselves of this pain until we elevate ourselves consciously out of the old ways of thinking that has kept us imprisoned for so long. It is time to unveil the illusion.

> *"That's why we are not discouraged. No, even if outwardly we are wearing out, inwardly we are being renewed each and every day. This light, temporary nature of our suffering is producing for us an everlasting weight of glory, far beyond any comparison, because we do not look for things*

that can be seen but for things that cannot be seen. For things that can be seen are temporary, but things that cannot be seen are eternal."

~ 2 CORINTHIANS *4:16-18 (NOG)*

The pain we experience in life is not the end of the road. It is a guide for those who can bear its cross because pain will always lead you to a greater place, if you let it. There are lessons tied to the pain and suffering that we experience. As we elevate our minds, releasing all negativity, we can begin the transformation of pain to power. Many people believe when you experience an immense amount of pain and suffering, that your power is taken away. On the contrary, the pain and suffering free you from the illusion of people. Huey P. Newton said, "Power is the ability to describe phenomena and make it act in a desired manner." Like a caged bird, you have grown stronger and are now ready to sing.

It is time to see through your pain. There is a demand within you to see something different. It is a calling that must be answered. What you do in the now creates possible outcomes for what will be. Intriguingly, as we create new thoughts, old thought processes become passé thus changing the course of our immediate future. This action yields a continuous change due to a changed thought process.

Your ability to adapt to change is best illustrated by how gracefully and optimistically you do so. As every moment in life passes, change occurs. The relativity of what we were, what we are, and what will be is constantly evolving. Heraclitus, a philosopher, states, "The only constant in life is change." We may further conclude that it is okay to change. Development and advancement are a part of God's process for our lives. By walking in our divine purpose, not only helps us experience happiness, but it transforms our pain to power.

This reminds me of a story about a master standing on the shore with two monks watching a red flag blowing in the wind. Each student sat patiently waiting to hear the master's instructions. He asked them as they watched the red flag blowing, "Is it the wind or the flag that moves?" One monk responded the wind and the other stated the flag. They were both right. Life standing still is relative to ongoing motion. What we perceive to be the truth, will be our truth. If we perceive that there is no end to suffering, then we will always suffer. However, if we learn from our hardships, we will outgrow our pain and turn it into power. As we experience pain and any that follows, we will understand it is for purpose. Do not let your pain break you, there is victory around the corner.

Unveiling the Illusion

*"A free bird leaps on the back of the
wind and floats downstream till the
current ends and dips his wing
in the orange sun rays and
dares to claim the sky.
But a bird that stalks down his narrow cage
can seldom see through his bars of rage
his wings are clipped and his feet are tied
so he opens his throat to sing."*

~ MAYA ANGELOU

Chapter 6

A Resilient Spirit

Dr. Melida A. Harris Barrow

"If you can't fly then run, if you can't run then walk, and if you can't walk then crawl; but whatever you do keep moving forward."

~Dr. Martin Luther King Jr.

Unveiling the Illusion

Sometimes the cares of this life weigh heavy upon our shoulders causing us to question our abilities. Truthfully speaking, life can be very hard. Each day we awaken with the best intentions to make the most of our time here on Earth. Unfortunately, things do not always go as planned. We encounter various roadblocks, which makes life too difficult to handle. There are times when the cares of life bring us to our knees and all we can do is crawl. The fact of the matter is that it does not matter how long it takes for you to accomplish your life's mission as long as you accomplish it. The race does not go to the fastest runner or the strongest competitor. It belongs to the person who has endurance. You have to push through no matter what life throws your way. No matter what you do in life, you cannot look back. Keep moving forward. Stay resilient!

"Facts do not cease to exist because they are ignored (Aldous Huxley)." Sadly, the truth is unfortunate things are going to happen to us all. If nothing has attempted to set you back, keep living. There will be situations and circumstances that are beyond our control. During these troublesome times, we have to learn how to deal with these problems. Faith will not change your reality. Ignoring the situation will not make it disappear into thin air. For some reason, we have adopted the mindset that if we ignore the problem it will go away in due time. Today, we have all types of vices that temporarily help us cope with issues like food, drugs, alcohol, etc. In fact, we get caught in a short-lived illusion, that it's okay. The truth of the matter is that if we do not address our issues or seek out a solution to resolve our problems, we will never overcome them. Until you realize that these problems do not define who you are, your problems will keep you in a vicious continuous cycle. You are running, but going nowhere. Stop the cycle. Adjust your way of thinking. The problem is not created to conquer you; you were created to conquer it. To every problem, there is a solution. Let your character speaks to being one who is tenacious and resilient.

I often find myself saying, "If you jump out of your dreams, the only place you will land is in other people's reality." This statement is true and definitely applicable to today's social structure. It identifies the psychological breakdown of people who have had an epiphany or conscious awakening to their situation. We must be awakened to a social reintegration, as our optimist love to call it, resiliency! Being resilient is having the ability to quickly recover from adverse situations that we encounter throughout life whether it is stress, illness, injury or behavioral modification.

I often think of the 'crab mentality'. The African America culture refers this mentality as being like 'crabs in a barrel' and often compare themselves by themselves as such. The analogy of this metaphor claims that people of the same race will attempt to diminish the importance of anyone else of that race that achieves success beyond others. In other words, they are held back, due to competitive jealousy, hatred, spite, etc. Is this your truth?

Question? Who owns the barrel? Who put the crabs in the barrel? Why do the crabs want to get out of the barrel? Did you ever consider crabs were never meant to be in a barrel? Is it wrong for all crabs in the barrel to want to be free at the same time? These are thought provoking questions that need to be considered and hopefully change the perspective about crabs being in a barrel. To me, each crab is resilient. They understand their purpose was never to be placed in a barrel piled on top of one another. Just like the crabs, we were never intended to be placed in a restrictive environment 'bunched together'. The results are detrimental for achieving freedom. Let me make it plain, it is human nature to be free. That is the way the God of the Universe created us. Don't believe the illusion that our own kind wants to annihilate us to make themselves better.

Being resilient requires you to quickly identify and address the problem. When we acknowledge our state of being and embrace it from a spiritual perspective, it will create a new outlook. Do not ever believe your situation defines who you are. We have to develop a resilient spirit that answers the call of God's purpose for our lives. We must reassure our purpose, sometimes out loud, to ourselves. Become refocused. Understanding that although I have encountered unfortunate experiences, I can unequivocally recover. Afterwards, I must further elongate that process by going the extra distance to encourage others that they too can recover or be free. What is designed to take us out of the race has actually equipped us mentally and spiritually for what's ahead. In the words of George Eliot, "It is never too late to be what you might have been."

> *"But, in life, it is not about how hard you can hit, it is about how hard you can get hit and keep moving forward."*
>
> ~ ROCKY BALBOA

Remember if you can't run then walk; if you can't walk then crawl; if you can't crawl then will yourself to move forward as Dr. King inspired us to do. No matter what happens in our life, the most important thing to remember is to keep advancing. In life, we will make mistakes over and over again, but never stop progressing, growing and evolving. Thomas Edison once stated, "I have not failed. I've found 10,000 ways that won't work."

Unveiling the Illusion

"Being resilient is embracing our imagination and creating what we envision. It is about walking with a mighty spirit, telling yourself that I am enough of an artist to draw freely upon my imagination. For imagination is more important than knowledge. Knowledge is limited, but my imagination encircles the world."

~ Albert Einstein

Being resilient is something that anyone of us can be. Life is hard, but our history is enriched with men and women who have stepped out on their resiliency to believe in their dreams to create a new world in a new age. Our nation is a shining example of resiliency. You are a shining example of that resiliency. I am a shining example of resiliency. Always remember, if a person truly wishes to fulfill their dreams, then unveil the illusion. Do not allow the reality of how the world sees you to become your reality.

Chapter 7

Success

Dr. Melida A. Harris Barrow

*"Success is not final; failure is not fatal:
it is the courage to continue that counts."*

~ WINSTON CHURCHILL

Unveiling the Illusion

Often, I think to myself, at what point do I spread the banner of success proudly across the front of my home like a child mesmerized at a deck of football cards on his bedroom floor? The moment I can say "I made it". This is a time we all fantasize as we commute to a place where we work tirelessly hoping to be rescued sooner than later. After all, what is life without success? Is our life's pursuit to become successful? How is success defined and who has done the defining? How do I know that I have arrived and what do I do when I arrive?

Success is never final! There should be no end to the milestones we cross in our life's journey. Yet, when success for your life is not defined by your own standards, success can be limited. The truth is, there are no limits. The only limits are those self-imposed. This can only be recognized when you understand the true meaning of success. Remember, it's how you define success for your life.

Man cannot define success for you and never could have, to be honest. Being successful does not come with a title, position, salary or place of residence. When you achieve levels given to you, this is not [REAL] success. This is standardization. You have exceeded the standard for what is expected of you based on what someone else thinks. You are limited by a man made formula that has calculated your worth. How is this possible? Is having a Mercedes Benz truly a status of success when you always wanted a Subaru?

Better yet, how can having a five-bedroom home with a pool be successful when I always wanted a log cabin? People have expensive cars with nowhere to go and a home with no one to love them. Is this success? I want you to take a moment and ask yourself, "What does success mean to me?"

> *"Success is not the key to happiness. Happiness is the key to success. If you love what you are doing, you will be successful."*
>
> ~ ALBERT SCHWEITZER

Sadly, most people will spend their entire lives helping someone else build their dreams, instead of building their own. If you ask someone who owns a company, how would you define success? Their answer would probably be something like this; it is doing what makes you happy every day. Day-after-day, CEOs and Entrepreneurs, come to work doing what they love to do. For them, it is not work, but an investment in themselves. Let us turn our attention and evaluate the person who works twelve hours a day for the man who owns the company. He is paid a six figure salary and has twenty vacation days annually and twenty sick days. That's pretty good, but he is working for the company. He is not fulfilling his vision or purpose. The worker is paid to be creative and assertive, but within the guidelines and demands of the company. If he crosses those lines, he can and will be replaced, regardless of the long hours and sacrifices he makes for the company. While twelve hours to the person who owns the company may seem like a few hours; twelve hours to this man working for the company feels like twenty. The man that works twelve hours for the company-his happiness is based on his success with the job (titles and salary), rather than the success and happiness of doing what he loves to do. One man is living his dreams building what he envisions, while the other person is assisting him in building it.

Now, everyone cannot own the company. Furthermore, just because you own the company, does not mean you are happy or successful. There are people who are happy not being the owner. Others love assisting others. For example, take a man who is not particularly happy with what he does, but he is happy for the resources it provides for his family. In his eyes, he can take care of his family. He is considered successful. This is still a fair and honest assessment. This is his definition of success. It does not matter if you are making ten dollars an hour or one hundred dollars per hour, your happiness defines your success. If your success in someone else's company does not define your happiness, then pursue what makes you genuinely happy.

Conclusion

This book was written to introduce to you the powers and knowledge that you already have once the illusion is removed. You do not need to seek what is already there. This written script was for me to highlight things that can change your life. It has changed mine. The world is a very vicious place and when you have learned to survive that is an amazing thing. The next step is to share your wisdom and knowledge through life's experiences. That is what I am doing in this manuscript.

I have read many stories about various countries and the many travesties that prey others. It is not right. There are times I wonder if this is not hell. When you observe the ill treatment of others, life seems too much to bear.

Slavery and the holocausts calamities are repeating itself all over again. What order do we have? Whose order are we under? Your life has been nothing but an illusion from the very beginning.

The way the world is today, we do not know if we will see tomorrow. It has become evident that we are under an illusion and must break free from it. If we do not, we will continue to succumb to this world's system. We are wasting away precious time. You are on autopilot because you have not discovered who you are or whose you are. Normalcy does not consist of being continuously depressed, disappointed, unhappy or miserable. This is not normal. Step out of the illusion and fight for your freedom. We are destined to win!

If I were to ask someone about their ancestor's history, they would not believe that it dates back to Africa. They would tell you, "I am from Panama." That is what the illusion has done to us. We believe what we are told. I hate to say, we do not explore or examine anything that can add value to our lives. Our fear to learn has become so great that we do not want to accept reality. We would rather deal with an illusion, accepting whatever has been told to us, than to break free and recognize our greatness. I understand that everyone will not embrace the truth; they don't want to.

Unveiling the Illusion

I want God's children to see what believing the illusion has done to them. It is time for us to seek the truth. In order for us to live the life that God has created us to live, it is necessary to find peace within ourselves. Knock on the door of your own life and experience love, truth and peace. Embrace the fullness of what God has created for all humanity. Break loose from the illusion created by man.

I would like to leave some inspirational words, quotes and biblical verses of wisdom that helped transition me from *the illusion* to living life to the fullest. It has changed my life forever.

1. Do not [EVER] give up! Keep moving forward.
2. Change your life today, not tomorrow.
3. Restore your mind and life.
4. Write an action plan for your life and make it happen.
5. Do not wait for someone to push you, push yourself.
6. Stop depending on others for your success.
7. Check and double-check your mindset! Check self, check your heart and check your beliefs.
8. Discover who you are. It is important for us to define ourselves and not look for others to define us.
9. Control your temper. There are people who create opportunities to provoke you to anger. Stay in control at all times.

10. Do not relinquish your power to others.
11. Strive for selflessness. There is no reward in life for being selfish, but there are numerous rewards for being selfless.
12. Strive to be a strategic thinker versus a conventional thinker.
13. Love yourself and others unconditionally! Love is important when it comes to changing your life. The more you love yourself and others unconditionally, the more peace and blessings will come to you.
14. Identify those people who create problems, friction and confusion; and separate yourself from naysayers.
15. Be a thinker.
16. Be wise. Wisdom gives you great insight to your surroundings.
17. Be slow to speak and quick to hear. Recognize that many of your battles are spiritual and not natural.
18. Include people in your journey, *but wisely!* You cannot take on your journey alone.
19. Listen to God! Listening is the key to prosperity and success.
20. Acknowledge all the gifts God gave you and use them.
21. Prioritize your life.

22. Do not become distracted with others. Stay the course. Be cautious about putting other people's project and aspiration before your own.
23. Do not allow past anger or pain to hold you hostage.
24. Do not fall into someone else's pain. It is okay to help people, but do not take on their issues and allow it to directly impact your life. Be their support, but not bear a false burden.
25. Acknowledge your past. You have to deal with your past in order to move forward or it will hold you in bondage and immobilize you.
26. Allow criticism to enlighten you, not negatively affect you. Analyze the different perspectives, but do not let it change you.
27. Be a light! You have a purpose. Do not let anyone devalue you or dim your light of success.
28. Fulfill your God given purpose. Your purpose was given to you by God. You should not allow your insecurity, jealousy, pettiness and hate to destroy it.

Mr. & Mrs. Felipe Barrow

"Because we unveiled and renewed our thoughts we are able to choose happiness instead of seeking or waiting to be happy."
~ Dr. Melida A. Harris Barrow

Live your life fully appreciating the moment. It will help you understand and fulfill your purpose.
~ Felipe A Barrow

Quotes

* "Don't let ego it will take you to a place of darkness. The ego seeks domination and power and when it's not accomplished, it leaves you feeling powerless. You don't need ego to be a powerful woman/man of God. You're powerful without it." ~ Dr. Melida A. Harris Barrow
* "Because I unveiled and renewed my thoughts I am able to choose happiness instead of seeking or waiting to be happy." ~ Dr. Melida A. Harris Barrow
* "Changing the world starts with changing ourselves and to change ourselves we need to change our mindset and uncover the illusion of this world. Ask yourselves these questions. Why are our

children killing each other? Why are prisons privatized? Why does racism exist? What makes you feel inferior to others? Why do we have reservations to work with each other? Why is the school system not teaching current world issues? It is time to stop acting on misinformation and find the truth that will change your life. It is time to activate the mind God gave you and the life He meant for you to live. It is time for a change." ~ Dr. Melida A. Harris Barrow

* "Racism is an illusion that exists only when you believe it. The antidote to that belief is to know who you are. Discovering yourself through the understanding of who you were created to be, is the greatest weapon against racism. No man is inferior or superior to another. We were all created in the likeness & image of God, with unique gifts and abilities to contribute to this world." ~ Dr. Melida A. Harris Barrow
* "The ability to effect change, rest in your GOD Giving Purpose." ~ Felipe A. Barrow
* "If you have time to whine and complain about something then you have the time to do something about it." ~ Anthony J. D'Angelo
* Never stop fighting until you arrive at your destined place-that is, the unique you. Have an aim in life, continuously acquire knowledge, work hard,

and have perseverance to realize the great life. ~ A. P. J. Abdul Kalam

* I tell my kids and I tell proteges, always have humility when you create and grace when you succeed, because it's not about you. You are a terminal for a higher power. As soon as you accept that, you can do it forever. ~ Quincy Jones
* "Positive thoughts are a source of joy, love and an indication of our alignment with the source. Negative thoughts create disharmony in our body for example depression, fear and aggression indicate misalignment with the source. ~ *Hina Hashmi*
* "The desire to have the power over others and dominate them arises basically from the negative thoughts that you have inside you." ~ Stephen Richards
* "A good friend who points out mistakes and imperfections and rebukes evil is to be respected as if he reveals a secret of hidden treasure." ~ Buddha
* "It is wrong to think that misfortunes come from the east or from the west; they originate within one's own mind. Therefore, it is foolish to guard against misfortunes from the external world and leave the inner mind uncontrolled." ~ Buddha
* "You yourself, as much as anybody in the entire universe, deserve your love and affection." – Buddha

* "However many holy words you read, However many you speak, What good will they do you If you do not act on upon them? ~ Buddha
* "Believe nothing, no matter where you read it, or who said it, no matter if I have said it, unless it agrees with your own reason and your own common sense. ~ Buddha

Unveiling the Illusion

Dr. Melida A. Harris Barrow

For God has not given us a spirit of fear, but of power and of love and of a sound mind.

~ 2 Timothy 1:7 (NKJV

Bible Verses

The "LORD" will fight for you; you need only to be still"

~ Exodus 14:14 (NIV)

Seek ye first the kingdom of God, and his righteousness; and all these things shall be added unto you.

~ *MATTHEW 6:33 (KJV)*

God created human beings in his own image. In the image of God he created them; male and female he created them.

~ Genesis 1:27

The one who gets wisdom loves life; the one who cherishes understanding will soon prosper.

~ Proverbs 19:8 (NIV)

For the Lord gives wisdom; from his mouth come knowledge and understanding. He holds success in store for the upright, he is a shield to those whose walk is blameless, for he guards the course of the just and protects the way of his faithful ones. Then you will understand what is right and just and fair every good path. For wisdom will enter your heart, and knowledge will be pleasant to your soul. Discretion will protect you, and understanding will guard you.

~ Proverbs 2: 6-11(NIV)

Do not withhold good from those to whom it is due, when it is in your power to act.
Do not say to your neighbor, "Come back tomorrow and I'll give it to you" when you already have it with you.
Do not plot harm against your neighbor, who lives trustfully near you.
Do not accuse anyone for no reason—when they have done you no harm.

~ Proverbs 3:27-30 (NIV)

Unveiling the Illusion

The righteous choose their friends carefully, but the way of the wicked leads them astray.

~ Proverbs 12:26 (NIV)

For the Spirit God gave us does not make us timid, but gives us power, love and self-discipline.

~ Timothy 1:7 (NIV)

Be on your guard; stand firm in the faith; be courageous; be strong.

~ 1 Corinthians 16:13 (NIV)

After this I saw another angel coming down from heaven. He had great authority, and the earth was illuminated by his splendor. With a mighty voice he shouted: " 'Fallen! Fallen is Babylon the Great! 'She has become a dwelling for demons and a haunt for every impure spirit, a haunt for every unclean bird, a haunt for every unclean and detestable animal. For all the nations have drunk the maddening wine of her adulteries. The kings of the earth committed adultery with her, and the merchants of the earth grew rich from her excessive luxuries." Then I heard another voice from heaven say: "Come out of her, my people,'so that you will not share in her sins, so that you will not receive any of her plagues; for her sins are piled up to heaven, and God has remembered her crimes. Give back to her as she has given; pay her back double for what she has done. Pour her a double portion from her own cup. Give her as much torment and grief as the glory and luxury she gave herself. In her heart she boasts, "I sit enthroned as queen. I am not a widow; I will never mourn." Therefore in one day her plagues will overtake her: death, mourning and famine. She will be consumed by fire, for mighty is the Lord God who judges her.

~ Revelation 18:1-8 (NIV)

Testimonials

Because of Dr. Melida Harris Barrow's Love, Truth and Peace Global Initiative, and the support and guidance I have received from her, I was finally able to embrace the gifts I have been given from Eternity and my Creator to develop. I firmly believe that God connects you with people who are meant to be in your life. Personally, I believe Dr. Melida Harris-Barrow is the person that God sent to help me, and guide me, as my mom would do, if she were alive. I know she is proud of me wherever she is.

Saludos cordials,
Leila Tamara Salazar Moreno
Presidente
ETHNICITIES Magazine

Dr. Melida A. Harris Barrow

I met Dr. Harris-Barrow two years ago at the Expocomer Trade Show in Panama City, Panama. Her beautiful spirit was the first thing I noticed. She is a multi-cultural powerhouse and international magnet. Her insight has opened the doors for so many entrepreneurs that were previously closed. THANK YOU, THANK YOU, THANK YOU!
Valerie Winfield, CEO
Val's Paper Passion

Thanks to Dr. Harris-Barrow and by God's grace, I began to discover that my illusion was a big lie, because this would never become my reality, nor did I actually want to be part of that world. Deep inside in my dreams we are still calling out and crying to be manifested. I discovered that this lie crippled me from living my dreams and loving myself. By running away from my dreams I was running away from myself. It was more painful not being myself. My past circumstances damaged my self-esteem and my self-image. Imprinted on my mind was that I was worthless and unable to achieve anything. Deep in my heart I knew that the person I dreamt of being, was the real me. Hiding inside of this broken woman I still had the desire to become that person. I started to evaluate myself and face my pains. Eventually, I granted myself grace. I realized it is not over until I give up. Thank you, Dr. Melida A. Harris Barrow for introducing Unveiling the Illusion: Know Who You Are.
Hanna Olmberg
Attorney at Law-Entrepreneur
Suriname

Unveiling the Illusion

The impact Dr. Melida Harris-Barrow has had in my life as my mentor has been phenomenal! She came into my life when I had just launched my life coaching business and in a little less than six months she had taken my mindset and faith to the next level. She instilled in me the real values of Love, Truth and Peace, which became the foundation of my business. Through her spiritual teachings I was able to connect deeper within myself, uncover more about myself and thus unleash the inner power that had been held within for so long. In addition, she nominated me an Honorary Doctorate Degree of Philosophy in Humanities. I will always be grateful. She will always be my mentor, spiritual mother, family and friend.

Dr. Lakisha Ross
President
Mindset Over Everything

Acknowledgements

This book is about my life's ventures. There are many people and family members from around the world that made an indelible impression on my life. Without them, this book could not have been written.

I come from a family of visionaries that is courageous and resilient. I owe this to my paternal grandmother from Jamaica, Eunice Brown and maternal grandparents from San Andres, Colombia, Ormie Rankin Davis and Arcelio Davis. Additionally, I am deeply appreciative to my beloved father, Reginaldo Keen Johnson (deceased) and mother, Merline M. Johnson for their love. I also extend special gratitude to my aunts and uncles, Mr. & Mrs. Melvin Belinfante, Mr. & Mrs. Olin Scott, and Mr. & Mrs. Arcelio (Jimmy) Davis.

I must send much love to Pastor Abraham Adesayo, Jane Patterson & family, my niece, Caressa Johnson & nephews, Alfredo Escalona, Jeremy Johnson and Reynaldo Johnson.

"Thank You" Judge Andre Harris lll for donating your kidney to me. These two words seem so inadequate for the gift of life you have given to me. March 16, 2017, will be15 years receiving this precious gift. May God continue to bless you and your family."

To my extended mothers & fathers who counseled and loved me throughout my life. For all of the good things I've done in life, they deserve much of the credit: Milray Leah Barrow, Albert S. Barrow, Arabella Fails, Judith Benoit, Ed Benoit, Edwin Ewen, Gladys Ewen, and Mildred Aikman (deceased). Thank you.

A special thank you to Rowena & Roberto Edwards, Dana Stannard, Reynaldo Ferdinand, Sebrina Baker and Marjorie Roc for their constant love and support throughout the years.

Last, but not least, this book took its first step for publication when I met Traneisha Jones. She provided steady counsel and guidance throughout this process. My beautiful sister-in-law, Michelle Johnson, who skillfully edited the book. And, I cannot forget Jannett Morrow, who guided me, as well as, provided information to self-publish this thought-provoking manuscript. Of course, the remarkable Love, Truth and Peace Inc. and Panama World

Trade & Investment Foundation Ambassadors that keep me grounded and inspired daily: Emelio Campbell, Dr. Jean Quijano, Alexander Adames, Yahalia Franklin, Yanis Chery, Julio Lezcano Guzmán, Georgeina Driver, Birdy Haggerty, Andrea Graham, Deon Lopez, Keila & Fausto Moreno, Ambassador Joseph Rankin, Valerie Winkfield, Lena Dixon, Dr. Pedrito Marrero, Ambassador Timothy Roland and Wanda Baez.

The Greatest Gift, Joy and Love of My Life, My Sons and Grandchildren.

I will be forever grateful Lord, for You gave me the Greatest Gift, the titles of Mother and Grandmother is unlike any title worth having.

This book may be purchased for educational, inspirational or ministry purposes.
The Author is available for speaking engagements, mentoring, individual coaching, seminars, workshops and corporate sessions.
For additional information on Dr. Harris Barrow and her line of products and services,
Visit: www. unveilingtheillusion.com
Email: melidabarrow@unveilingtheillusion.com or melida barrow14@gmail.com
Contact Information:
1-(954)-253-4656 (USA) or +507-832-0191 (Panama)

Notes

Notes

Notes

Notes

Notes

Notes

www.ingramcontent.com/pod-product-compliance
Lightning Source LLC
Chambersburg PA
CBHW071141090426
42736CB00012B/2193